Ultimate FACTIVITY Collection
HUMAN BODY

W9-ABA-005

DK | Penguin
Random
House

Senior Designer Clare Shedden
Editors Toby Mann, Laura Palosuo
Designers Wendy Bartlet, Charlotte Bull, Charlotte Milner,
Hannah Moore, Pamela Shiels, Sadie Thomas
Assistant Editor Sophia Danielsson-Waters
US Editor Margaret Parrish
US Senior Editor Shannon Beatty
Consultant Steve Parker
Jacket Art Editors Holly Jackman, Amy Keast, Charlotte Milner
Illustrators Wendy Bartlet, Charlotte Bull, Chris Howker,
Jake McDonald, Charlotte Milner, Clare Shedden, Sadie Thomas
Senior Pre-Production Producer Tony Phipps
Producer Leila Green
Creative Technical Support Sonia Charbonnier
Managing Editor Penny Smith
Managing Art Editors Marianne Markham, Gemma Glover
Publisher Mary Ling
Creative Director Jane Bull

First American Edition, 2016
This edition published in the United States in 2016 by
DK Publishing, 345 Hudson Street, New York, New York 10014

A catalog record for this book is available from the Library of Congress
ISBN: 978-1-4654-4506-3

DK books are available at special discounts when purchased in bulk for sales promotions,
premiums, fund-raising, or educational use. For details, contact:
DK Publishing Special Markets, 345 Hudon Street, New York, New York 10014 or SpecialSales@dk.com.
Printed and bound in China by L. Rex Printing Co., Ltd.
All images © Dorling Kindersley Limited
For further information see www.dkimages.com

A WORLD OF IDEAS:
SEE ALL THERE IS TO KNOW
Discover more at **www.dk.com**

All systems go

The human body is an amazing machine. It is made up of different parts, all working together. The parts make up the systems that support, protect, control, and feed the body.

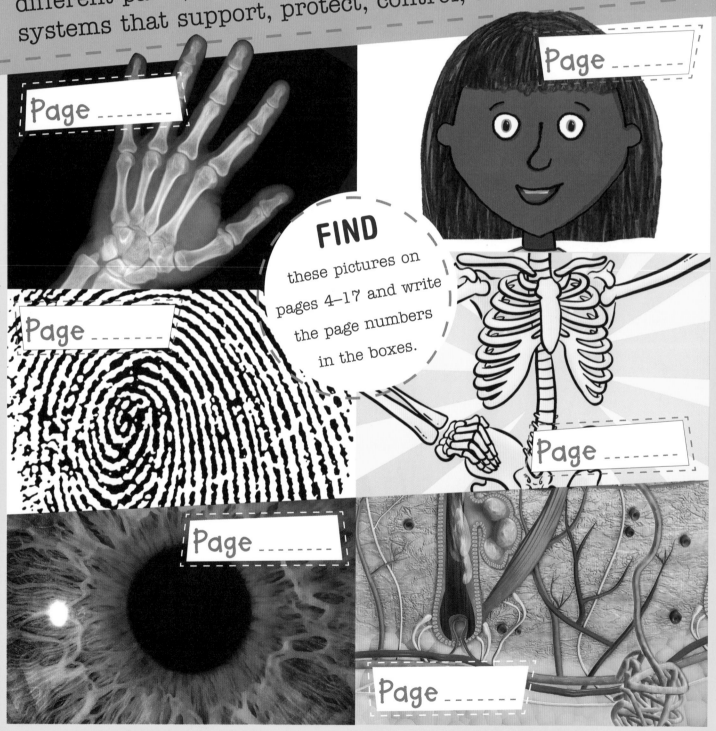

Page _____

Page _____

Page _____

FIND these pictures on pages 4–17 and write the page numbers in the boxes.

Page _____

Page _____

Page _____

Amazing human quiz

Test your knowledge with this fun quiz and learn about the wonders of the human body—from blood to brains. Discover the strength of the liquid in your stomach and the sensitivity of your skin.

ANSWER whether you think each statement is true or false.

1 Messages from the brain can travel at speeds up to 900mph (1,500kph) between **nerve cells**.

TRUE ○ ○ FALSE

Nerve cells send messages through electrical impulses.

2 Over a lifetime, the human heart will pump 52 million gallons (200 million liters) of blood.

TRUE ○ ○ FALSE

The heart is made of a specialized muscle that never gets tired.

3 Stomach acids are so strong that your body has to replace the lining of your stomach once an hour.

TRUE ○ ○ FALSE

4 If stretched out flat, a rat's brain would be the size of a postage stamp, a chimpanzee's the size of a book, and a human's the size of a tabloid newspaper.

TRUE ○ ○ FALSE

1st Brain

Once upon a time, there was a very smart chimpanzee...

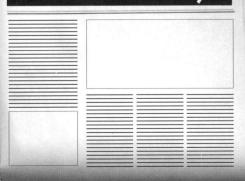

Human Weekly

5 Human fingers are so sensitive that if they were the size of Earth, they'd be able to feel the difference between a house and a car.

TRUE ○ ○ FALSE

WITNESS THE HUMAN BODY'S STRONG BONES

STICK
the missing bone stickers in place on the skeleton.

Your bones give your body its shape. Without them you'd be floppy and wouldn't be able to stand or lift your arms or legs.

Skull
The skull protects your brain.

Mandible
Your mandible (lower jaw) is hinged to your skull so you can open your mouth.

Radius & Ulna
There are two bones in your lower arm, the radius and the ulna. If there were only one bone there you wouldn't be able to turn your wrist.

Sternum
You can feel this hard bone at the center of your chest.

Ribs
The rib cage protects your vital organs—the heart and the lungs.

Clavicle
This bone is also known as the collarbone.

Humerus
It's not your funny bone (even if it sounds like it should be). The funny bone is actually a nerve going past your humerus.

Spine
Your spine is made up of lots of small bones called "vertebrae" (vur-tuh-brey).

Pelvis
Your pelvis is made of lots of smaller bones that join together into an adult. as you grow into an adult.

Hand

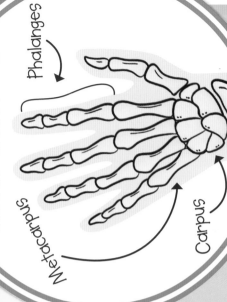

Each hand contains 27 bones!

Phalanges

Phalanges

Metacarpus

Carpus

Phalanges
Phalanges is the name of the bones in your fingers and toes.

Femur
This is the longest and strongest bone in your body!

Patella
The patella is also known as the kneecap. You can feel it on the front of your knee.

Tibia
The tibia is the larger of the two bones in your lower leg.

Metatarsus
These bones are found across the middle of your foot.

Ulna
The ulna is the bigger of the two bones in your forearm.

Bone facts
Babies are born with 350 different bones, but adults have only 206. Some of your smaller bones join together as you grow.

Over half of an adult's bones are found in their hands and feet (106 out of 206).

Fibula
Like your lower arm, your lower leg also has two bones: the tibia and the fibula.

Tarsus
This group of bones makes up the back of your foot and your heel.

Organize your Organs

Your organs all have jobs to perform to keep you alive. These are the main organs in your body—do you know what they do?

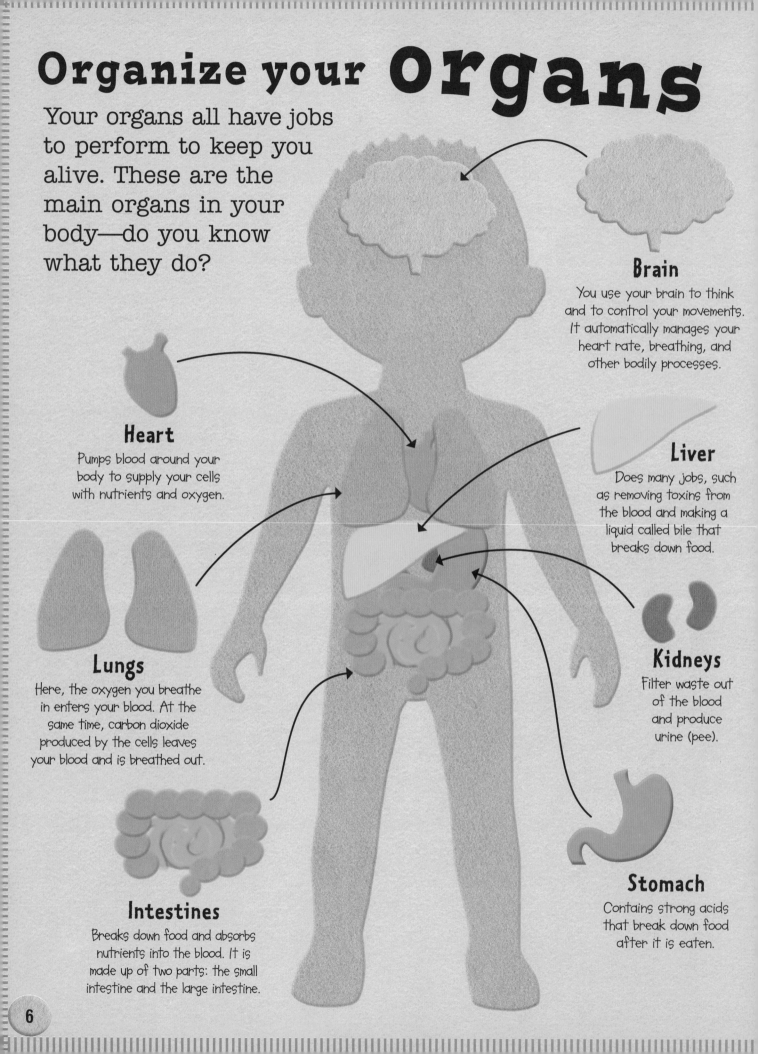

Brain
You use your brain to think and to control your movements. It automatically manages your heart rate, breathing, and other bodily processes.

Heart
Pumps blood around your body to supply your cells with nutrients and oxygen.

Liver
Does many jobs, such as removing toxins from the blood and making a liquid called bile that breaks down food.

Lungs
Here, the oxygen you breathe in enters your blood. At the same time, carbon dioxide produced by the cells leaves your blood and is breathed out.

Kidneys
Filter waste out of the blood and produce urine (pee).

Intestines
Breaks down food and absorbs nutrients into the blood. It is made up of two parts: the small intestine and the large intestine.

Stomach
Contains strong acids that break down food after it is eaten.

now your turn...

Squished in

Most organs are found in the torso (between the shoulders and pelvis). They are tightly packed together so that they all fit inside the body.

Test Your Knowledge

STICK all of the organ stickers in the correct place. Top tip: start with the kidneys.

Heart

Is about the size of a fist and fits between the lungs.

Brain

Fits inside the skull.

Start here!

Kidneys

Are right at the back behind the liver and stomach.

Lungs

Go around the heart.

Stomach

Goes behind the liver on the left-hand side of the body.

Liver

Sits in front of the stomach on the right-hand side of the body.

TRUE OR FALSE?

When an important person in ancient Egypt died their organs would be removed and buried with them in jars.

Intestines

Are long and thin, but are all squished together. They belong underneath the stomach and liver.

Hardworking cells

Your body contains lots of different types of cell, which all have their own roles. They are working together constantly to keep us alive. Here they are in action.

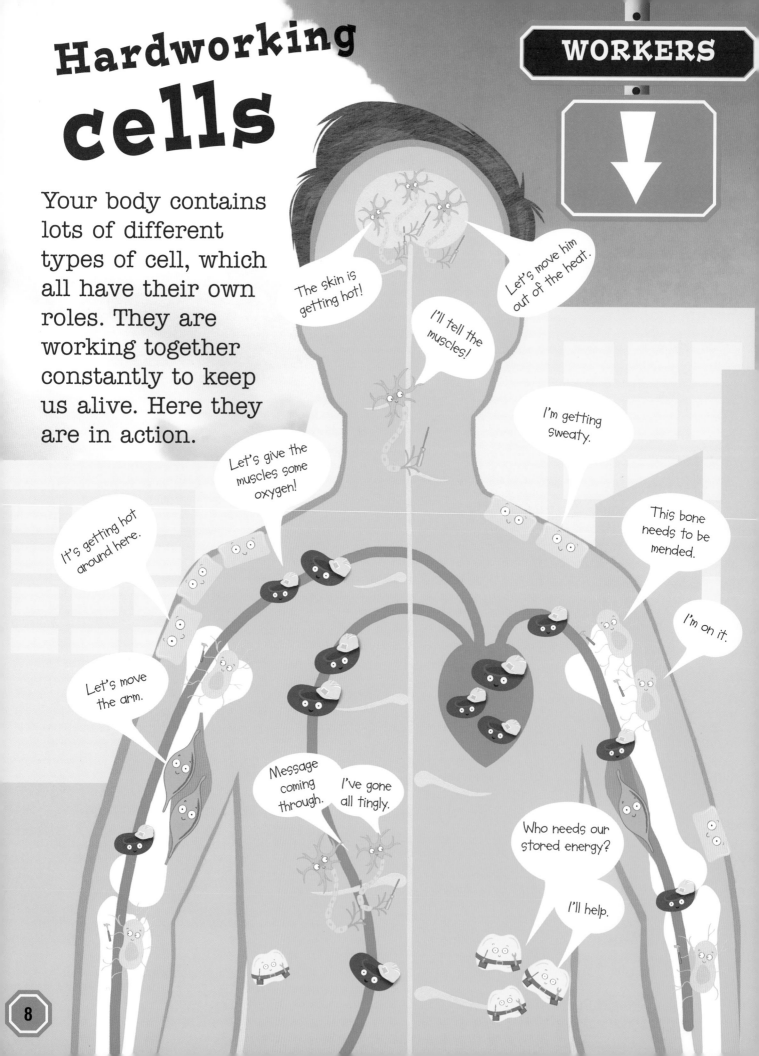

STICK

in the correct sticker for each cell. Use the shapes to help you.

Reporting to work

Blood cell

DEPARTMENT:

Oxygen delivery

ROLE:

Collects oxygen from the lungs and delivers oxygen and nutrients to cells around the body.

Bone cell

DEPARTMENT:

Construction

ROLE:

Produces the hard substance that our bones are made from.

Nerve cell

DEPARTMENT:

Internal communication

ROLE:

Delivers messages between the brain and all other parts of the body.

Muscle cell

DEPARTMENT:

Movement management

ROLE:

Forms long strings of cells that make up muscles. Contracts as needed.

Skin cell

DEPARTMENT:

Body protection, Data collection

ROLE:

Forms a protective barrier for the body. Reports on sensations from the outside world.

Fat cell

DEPARTMENT:

Energy supply, Insulation

ROLE:

Insulates body and stores energy to be used up by the muscles and organs.

All about skin

Your skin covers your entire body. It contains many types of cell, which do lots of different jobs. It is thicker and stretchier in some areas of your body than in others, and it can even change color!

Skin is your biggest organ! If you could stretch your skin out flat it would cover about 2½ square feet (2 square meters).

Which one does the skin NOT do?

TEST yourself on how much you know about skin and hair.

Three layers

There are three main layers to the skin. Each contains different types of cells and has different functions.

On top is the **epidermis** (ep–a–dur–mis). This layer is the outer barrier of your body. It is mostly made up of dead skin cells.

Next is the **dermis** (dur–mis). This contains hair follicles, blood vessels, touch sensors, and sweat glands.

Last is the **subcutaneous** (sub–kew–TAY–nee–us) **tissue**. It is made up of fat storage cells.

What does skin do for us?

One of these facts is incorrect. Can you spot which?

1. It stores fat and water.

2. It produces sweat and changes the blood flow to help you cool down.

3. It stops too much water from getting into or escaping your body.

4. It stops germs from getting inside you.

5. It produces light so that you can glow in the dark.

6. It filters some of the sun's harmful rays.

7. It allows you to sense temperature and the things that you touch.

8. It removes toxins from your body by adding them to your sweat.

Which one is the fake fact?

1 You lose about 35,000 dead skin cells every hour.

TRUE FALSE

2 Around 1 trillion (1,000,000,000,000) bacteria are living on your skin.

TRUE FALSE

3 Lips are pink because they contain lots of a color pigment called melanin (mell-ah-nin).

TRUE FALSE

Skinny facts

Your skin varies in thickness. It is thinnest on your eyelids, where the dermis and epidermis are $\frac{1}{125}$ inch (0.2mm), and thickest on the soles of your feet, where they are $\frac{1}{8}$ inch (3mm).

4 You skin replaces all of its cells over the course of one year.

TRUE FALSE

Can you see the grooves in your finger print?

5 As much as 50 percent or more of the dust in your house is dead skin cells.

TRUE FALSE

6 Your skin makes up 15 percent of your total body weight.

TRUE FALSE

7 Our hair and nails are made out of a dead material called keratin (care-a-tin).

TRUE FALSE

8 Hair grows back faster and thicker if you cut it.

TRUE FALSE

Stick in the faces for each emotion

Fear

People expressing fear have upturned eyebrows, wide eyes, and open mouths.

Happiness

When happy, a person will raise the corners of his or her mouth into a smile.

Anger

Look for lowered eyebrows and bared teeth (or sometimes lips pressed together.)

STICK in face stickers that match the emotions above. Then draw the expressions below.

It's all over your face!

Sometimes we can tell how a person is feeling from the expression on their face. This is us communicating with other people without even speaking!

See if you can draw a face showing each emotion. Make sure to color it in afterward!

Write in the emotion you have drawn

I feel _____

I feel _____

I feel _____

Sadness

When sad, your jaw comes up and the corners of your mouth turn down into a frown.

Surprise

Look for raised eyebrows and a wrinkled forehead. The person may let out a gasp.

Disgust

A disgusted person will have a wrinkled nose, distorted mouth, and may raise one eyebrow.

A smile is a way of saying "hello" in any language.

A smile a day...

Smiling can make you feel happier and frowning can make you feel sadder, so make sure to keep on smiling!

Facts about... Expressions

Some scientists believe that everyone around the world uses the same **facial expressions**. How obvious a person's expressions are may depend on their culture.

I feel _____

I feel _____

I feel _____

What makes me, me?

Although we are all human, we have features that are unique only to us. Here are some things that make you different from anyone else and can even be used to identify you.

READ about the features unique to you and then complete the activities.

Facts about...

Unique prints

It's not just your fingers that have prints unique to you, your tongue and ear prints are also different from anyone else's.

Your iris

The iris (the colored part of your eye) has a unique pattern. This magnified image shows how detailed the pattern can be.

The black circle at the center of the eye is the pupil.

The iris is the colored section of the eye.

Handwriting

Everyone has slightly different handwriting, even if some people's look the same. Signatures (the way someone writes their own name), are used as a form of identiication.

This shows the signature of Elizabeth I (she was Queen of England between 1558 and 1603).

Write your signature here: _____

14

Face recognition

Special machines can recognize a person's face in real life and even from a photograph. You might see these machines at security checks, like those used at airports.

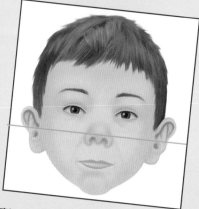

The machine scans the photograph and then compares it to the image it takes of the person standing in front of it.

Draw a picture of your face!

Fingerprints

Everyone has a unique set of fingerprints, even identical twins! Here are three examples of different types of prints. Can you see any of these shapes on your own fingertips?

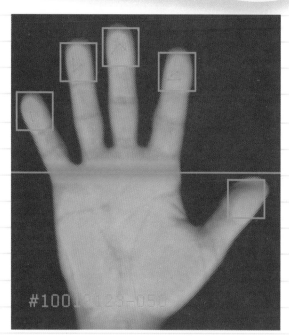

Loops enter from one side and curve around in a "U" shape back over to the side they started.

Whorls form a circular or spiral pattern, curving into the center.

Arches enter from one side, curve upward into an arch, and end on the opposite side.

This fingerprint scanner looks for key features of a fingerprint and measures the distances between them.

15

X-rays

OFF | ON

"X-rays" are a type of radiation. They allow us to see bones, organs, and teeth in the human body. A machine sends rays through the body that are then recorded as an image.

FIND the X-ray stickers for each body part and stick them in place.

You need to be still for a clear image to be taken.

Joints occur when two or more bones come in close contact.

Hand: The first-ever X-ray was of Wilhelm Röentgen's wife's left hand. He discovered X-rays in 1895.

Ankle: The ankle is a "hinge joint" that allows your foot to move freely.

Skull: The skull is made up of several bones that form a solid structure.

The elbow is one of the largest joints in the body and is very sturdy.

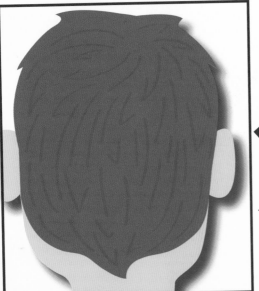

This is a fully formed skull. Babies' skull bones don't fuse until they're 18 months old.

Elbow: Three bones come together to form the elbow joint.

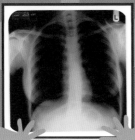

The symbol "X" stands for unknown. Röentgen didn't know what caused the rays.

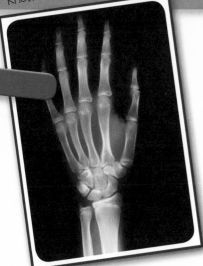

Draw and **COLOR** in the face and the body. You could make it look like you or someone you know.

This X-ray was taken of a mom, dad, boy, and girl. It's a fun take on a family photo.

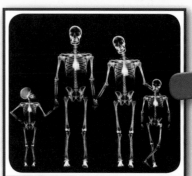

The letter "L" or "R" is used to show which way around the X-ray was taken.

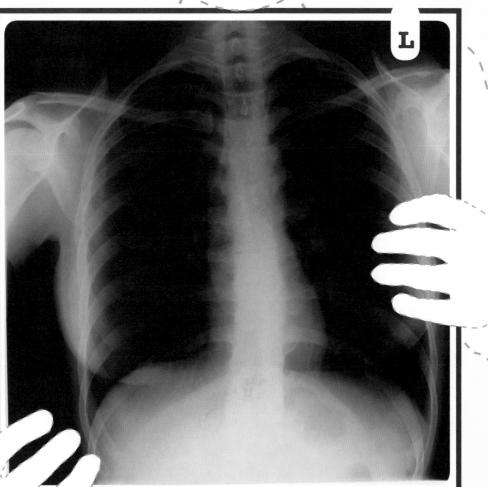

Chest: This x-ray is of the chest. It shows the spine, rib cage, and shoulders.

OFF ON

Insides out

There's a lot going on inside your body that you may not even realize! In this chapter we'll explore what your body does automatically, like pumping blood and using energy.

Don't forget to put your stickers in first.

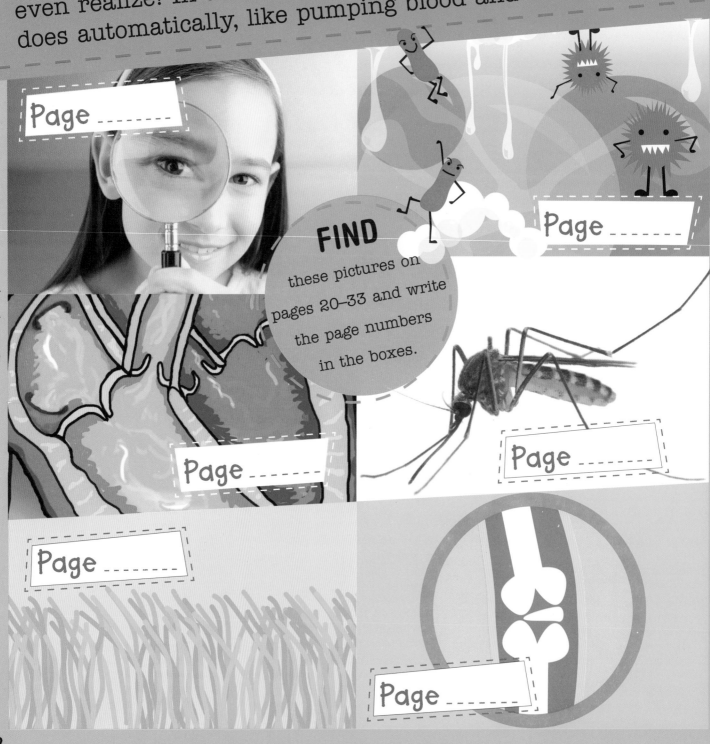

Page _____

Page _____

FIND these pictures on pages 20–33 and write the page numbers in the boxes.

Page _____

Page _____

Page _____

Page _____

READ

READ about how cells get their energy and color the image.

Charging the batteries

Your cells are like tiny power stations inside your body. Ever wondered why you need to breathe and eat food? That's because these are the fuels your cells use for energy.

Food

Oxygen

Your **food** is broken down by the digestive system into tiny particles so that your cells can absorb it.

Oxygen and food are absorbed by the blood and pumped around the body by your heart.

Dont forget to color in the batteries so they are fully charged with energy!

Oxygen is found in the air you breathe. It is separated from the other gases in the air by your lungs.

Muscle cell

Bone cell

Skin cell

Inside your cells the oxygen and food are turned into **energy**.

Each cell needs energy to be able to do its job.

Your body produces 3 MILLION new red blood cells every second.

Muscles

Your blood delivers oxygen and nutrients to the muscles. Cells in the muscles use these substances to produce energy and waste products.

Kidney

Intestines

Blood cells collect nutrients from food that is broken down in your intestines.

Kidney

In your liver and kidneys, toxins and waste products are filtered out of your blood.

Bone marrow

Red blood cells are created in the bone marrow.

In one day a red blood cell travels 12,000 miles (19,300 km) around your body.

There are almost 60,000 miles (100,000 km) of blood vessels in your body. (Enough to circle the Earth twice!)

STICK the puzzle pieces in place using the image on the left page as a guide.

Your amazing heart

Your heart is a superpowerful pump. Its job is to push blood around your body, delivering essential oxygen to all your cells.

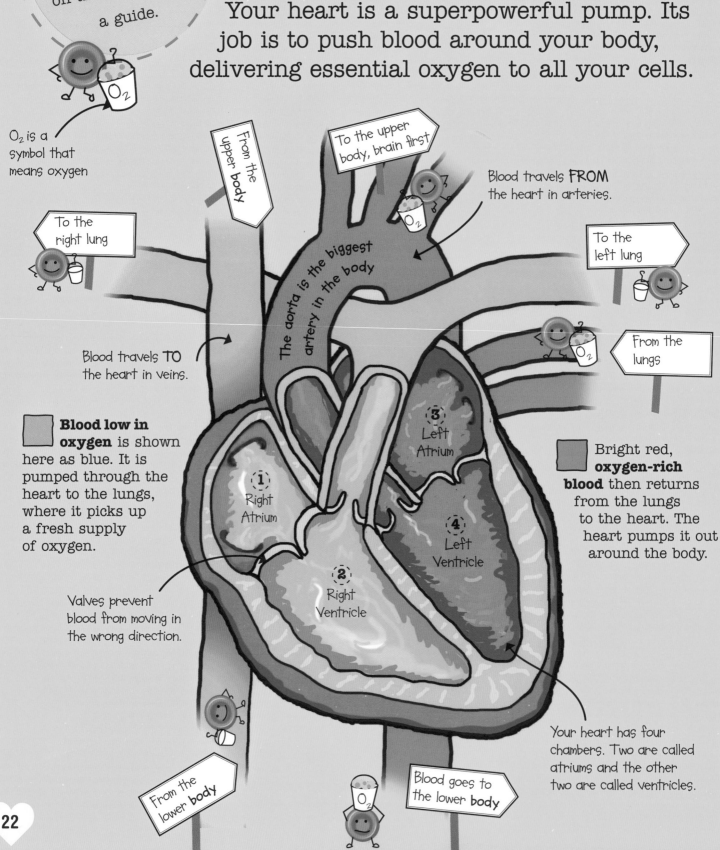

O_2 is a symbol that means oxygen

From the upper **body**

To the upper body, brain first

Blood travels **FROM** the heart in arteries.

To the right lung

To the left lung

The aorta is the biggest artery in the body

From the lungs

Blood travels **TO** the heart in veins.

Blood low in oxygen is shown here as blue. It is pumped through the heart to the lungs, where it picks up a fresh supply of oxygen.

① Right Atrium

② Right Ventricle

③ Left Atrium

④ Left Ventricle

Bright red, **oxygen-rich blood** then returns from the lungs to the heart. The heart pumps it out around the body.

Valves prevent blood from moving in the wrong direction.

From the lower **body**

Blood goes to the lower **body**

Your heart has four chambers. Two are called atriums and the other two are called ventricles.

HEART QUIZ

1 The average person's heart beats 70 times in one minute.

TRUE   FALSE

2 A baby's heart beats faster than an adult's.

TRUE   FALSE

3 Your blood is blue when not carrying oxygen.

TRUE   FALSE

4 An adult's heart can pump around 1,800 gallons (8,000 liters) of blood per day.

TRUE   FALSE

5 People who do a lot of exercise (like athletes) have a faster heart rate than normal when resting.

TRUE   FALSE

Now use the stickers to complete the picture and see how the blood flows through the heart

Take your pulse

Your arteries expand as your heart beats. You can feel one expanding if you press your fingers against your wrist. Count the pulses to find out how many times your heart beats per minute.

What's your heart rate?

_____ beats per minute

23

Breathe in!

You can go without many things for a few hours—chatting, reading, and even eating. But one thing you always need is oxygen. The lungs take it in from the air you breathe.

Breathing in and out

A sheet of muscle called the diaphragm helps get air to the lungs. Put your hand on your chest. Breathe in (inhale) and out (exhale). Can you feel what happens?

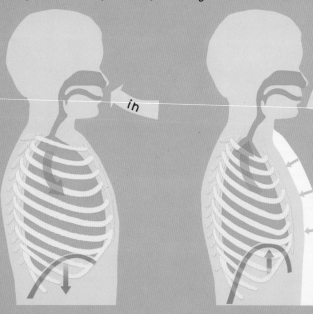

in

out

As you inhale, the diaphragm moves down. The lungs fill with air, pushing the chest out.

When you exhale, the diaphragm lifts up. This squashes the lungs to release air through the mouth.

Lungs

The lungs are surrounded by the rib cage and protected by it. Their job is to bring in **oxygen** and get rid of **carbon dioxide**. Oxygen keeps cells alive and is used by the body for energy, but carbon dioxide is a waste product.

The dome-shaped diaphragm is stretchy and moves up and down. It's a bit like a mini trampoline!

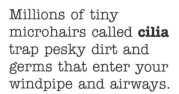

Millions of tiny microhairs called **cilia** trap pesky dirt and germs that enter your windpipe and airways.

Windpipe

Air travels to your lungs through the **windpipe**. The stiff rings in its wall keep it open so that air can always get through.

Bronchioles

Next, air flows into even smaller branches called **bronchioles**. You have around 30,000 in each lung!

Millions of mini air sacs—**alveoli**—are at the end of the bronchioles. Blood vessels surround them.

Air sacs

Bronchus

From the windpipe, the air enters each **bronchus.** This is a big airway branch that goes to one of the two lungs.

Did you know? The left lung is smaller than the right because it has to make room for the heart.

Oxygen

Oxygen passes from the alveoli into the blood stream, where it is picked up by red blood cells. Carbon dioxide leaves the lungs here, too.

25

Food processor

It takes around 1½ days for food to travel through the body. Find some counters and a die and see if you can get through the digestive system any quicker!

Start

Indigestion. Skip a turn.

10

9

Yogurt provides friendly bacteria. Move on three spaces!

8

7

Villi (vil—eye) are tiny, finger-shaped structures inside our small intestine. They help you absorb nutrients more efficiently.

11

12

13 Villi help you absorb nutrients. Move on a space!

Small intestine

The small intestine is a long, narrow tube where the nutrients from our food are absorbed. It is all squashed together to fit inside the body.

You will eat **30 tons** of food in your lifetime.

Rice

24

23 You've eaten too much. Go back two spaces!

22 Lack of fiber slows digestic Skip a turn.

How long?

Facts about...

If you stretched out your digestive system into a straight line it would be 30ft (9m) long—that's almost as long as a bus!

25

26 Not enough water. Go back one space.

27

1 **Saliva** breaks down food, go forward two spaces!

2 **Down** the wrong hole, go back to the start!

3

Food is pushed through our digestive system by your muscles. This is called **peristalsis** (per-uh-stal-sis).

4 Peristalsis moves food onward. Roll again!

6 Bad bacteria makes you sick. Go back three spaces!

Stomach

5 You've fallen into stomach acid, go forward two spaces!

When you blush, your stomach blushes too!

This is where stomach acid breaks down our food so it can be digested.

14

15 Spicy food! Move on two spaces.

16

17

Farts are made up of air we swallow and smelly gases released by bacteria.

Large intestine

By the time food reaches the large intestine, all the nutrients have been absorbed. Here the body takes most remaining water out of the leftovers.

18

21

20

19 Beans produce smelly gases. Move back one space.

28 You've eaten your vegetables. Move forward one space.

29

30 Restroom line. Skip a turn.

End

Mighty muscles

FIND the stickers for each type of muscle and stick them in place.

When something in the body moves, there is normally a muscle causing it. There are three main types of muscle, each found in different parts of the body.

Cardiac muscle

The muscle in the heart is different from muscles in the rest of the body. This is because it has to work every moment of our lives (from when we are born to when we die).

The heart is the only part of the body to contain cardiac muscle.

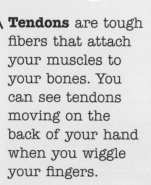

Tendons are tough fibers that attach your muscles to your bones. You can see tendons moving on the back of your hand when you wiggle your fingers.

Smooth muscles

Smooth muscles are found inside your organs. Normally, they work automatically and are controlled by your brain without you thinking about it.

Smooth muscles in your **eyes** allow the eye to focus. They also control the size of your pupils.

You have smooth muscles in your **intestines** to push your food through your body so it can be digested.

Skeletal muscles

Skeletal muscles are the muscles that you control yourself. They are often found in groups across the body.

You use your **facial muscles** to smile or frown, stick out your tongue, or make funny faces.

The **biceps** and **triceps** are found in your upper arms. You use them whenever you move your arms (like when you play tennis).

The main muscles in your legs are the **quadriceps** and the **hamstrings**. These are really useful for walking and running!

How do muscles make you move?

Contract

Relax

When you want to bend your arm, your **biceps** contracts, pulling your lower arm inward.

Your muscles can't push, they can only contract (pull) and relax. Most muscles work in pairs, one pulling in the opposite direction from the other.

Relax

Contract

When you want to straighten your arm, your **triceps** contracts, pulling your arm straight.

29

Body of water

Water makes up about 65 percent of your body. It plays an important role in the way your different body parts work, so make sure to drink plenty.

BRAIN

Drinking enough water makes your brain react faster and even improves your memory! About 75 percent of your brain is water.

BLOOD

Water dilutes your blood, allowing it to travel around your body easily. Around 90 percent of your blood is water.

LUNGS

Water keeps the lungs moist, making it is easier for you to breathe. Your lungs are about 85 percent water.

Facts about...

Where is it from?

About 60 percent of the water in your body comes from **drinking** (that's why it's important to drink enough). Your **cells** produce a small amount of water when they make energy, and the rest is absorbed from your **food.**

BONES

Your bones are about 20 percent water. Water also helps cushion your joints so they don't wear down.

STICK

the missing stickers in place. Use the colors to help you.

MUSCLES

Water keeps all of the tissues in your body moist—including muscle tissue! Your muscles are about 80 percent water.

SKIN

To help you cool down, your skin produces sweat (which is mostly water). Your skin is about 65 percent water.

5 Drinking too little water improves your memory.

TRUE   FALSE

4 Water makes up **around 90 percent** of your blood.

TRUE   FALSE

3 Sweat is made **entirely** from water.

TRUE   FALSE

2 Drinking enough water helps you breathe more easily.

TRUE   FALSE

1 Water makes up **around 75 percent** of the brain.

TRUE   FALSE

Too hot!

When it's hot out or you've been exercising, various body processes bring down your temperature quickly.

In the hot sun, a hat provides shade.

When sweat evaporates from your skin, it takes some heat with it.

Red cheeks and panting are ways of removing more heat.

Perfect temperature

The perfect temperature for your body to work as it should is 98.6°F (37°C). Your body works hard to keep your temperature as close to this as possible.

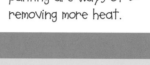

37°C

STICK
in the stickers to show how your body warms up and cools down.

Too cold!

Extra clothes help keep you warm.

Blood vessels on your skin get smaller to stop heat from leaving.

When you're cold, your body has ways of getting you warmed up again.

Shivering is your body's way of creating more heat.

Your hairs stand on end to trap heat near your skin.

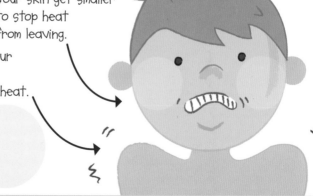

Draw yourself in these scenes and **COLOR** them in. What will you be wearing on a hot day? What about a cold one?

Good sensations

During our lives we are constantly sensing things in the world outside our bodies. In this chapter we will explore how our body works out what's going on around us.

Don't forget to put your stickers in first.

Page _____

Page _____

Page _____

FIND these pictures on pages 36–49 and write the page numbers in the boxes.

Page _____

Page _____

Page _____

The five main senses

Hello! My name is Aristotle (ah-ri-stot-ul). I lived around 2,400 years ago in ancient Greece. I was the first person to name the five main senses. People have been using these five names (or versions in their own languages) ever since.

Help this pear see, hear, taste, smell, and touch.

1 Sight (eyes)
Your eyes allow you to see. You can only see things that you eyes are pointing at.

2 Hearing (ears)
You use your ears to hear. You have them on either side of your head so you can hear all around you.

3 Taste (tongue)
Sweet, sour, bitter, salty, and savory—these are all sensations that your tongue can tell you about things you eat.

STICK
the body part stickers onto the pear.

4 Smell (nose)
Your sense of smell is provided by your nose. The closer something is to your nose, the easier it is to smell.

5 Touch (skin)
Wherever on your body something touches you, you can feel it. this is because you have touch receptors in your skin.

There are more than 20 different body parts to choose from!

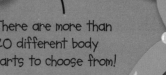

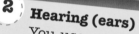

35

Your brain uses 20–25 percent of the energy your body produces.

On average, a human brain has 100 billion (100,000,000,000) neurons.

READ about the different parts of the brain and find them in the image. Then color them in.

The nervous system

The **nerves** are the cables that connect the different parts of the body to the brain via the spine. They are made up of long, thin cells called **neurons** that can pass on messages in the form of electrical signals. This network of connections is called **the nervous system**.

Movement

All of your deliberate movement starts in your brain. The brain sends messages to your muscles telling them to contract (pull) or relax.

Thinking

Creative and logical thinking take place in the brain. Our ability to find creative solutions to problems is one of the features that makes us human.

Memory

Your brain stores up memories of your life. Particularly strong memories are often associated with an image, smell, or emotion.

Emotion

Emotions originate in the brain. They can often have an effect on other parts of the body—such as when you blush because you are embarrassed.

The senses

There are different parts of the brain to process different senses. Sight and smell have their own separate sections.

Language

This part of the brain is where you form words and sentences. It is also where you make sense of the speech you hear and writing you read.

Can you find these objects in the different parts of the brain?

Automatic activity

Much of what your body does happens without you thinking about it. Examples are breathing, heartbeat, digestion, and temperature control.

Brain power

There is always a lot going on inside the brain, even when you are asleep! To make sure everything gets done, the brain is divided into sections that perform different tasks.

Trick of the eye

Your eyes and brain work together to figure out what you're seeing. Some images play tricks on the brain so that it misinterprets them. These are called **optical illusions.**

Are the horizontal lines straight?

Can you see dots between the crosses?

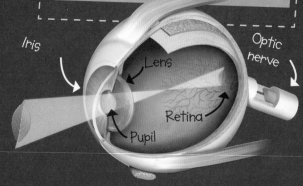

Iris

Lens

Optic nerve

Retina

Pupil

Much of what you see is filled in by your brain. Optical illusions work because they don't show what your brain expects to see.

Are the pink circles the same size?

Do the edges of the square look straight?

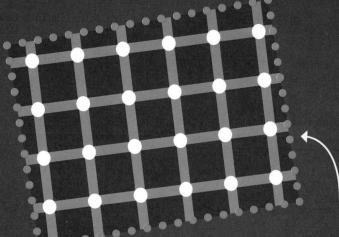

Can you see black dots in the white circles?

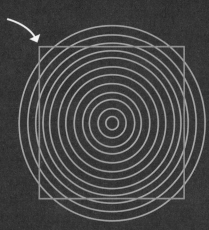

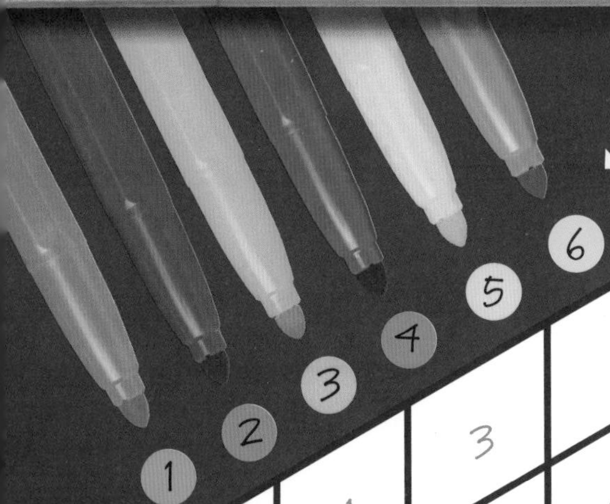

Use felt-tip pens to color the picture.

COLOR in the pattern by following the color key on the left.

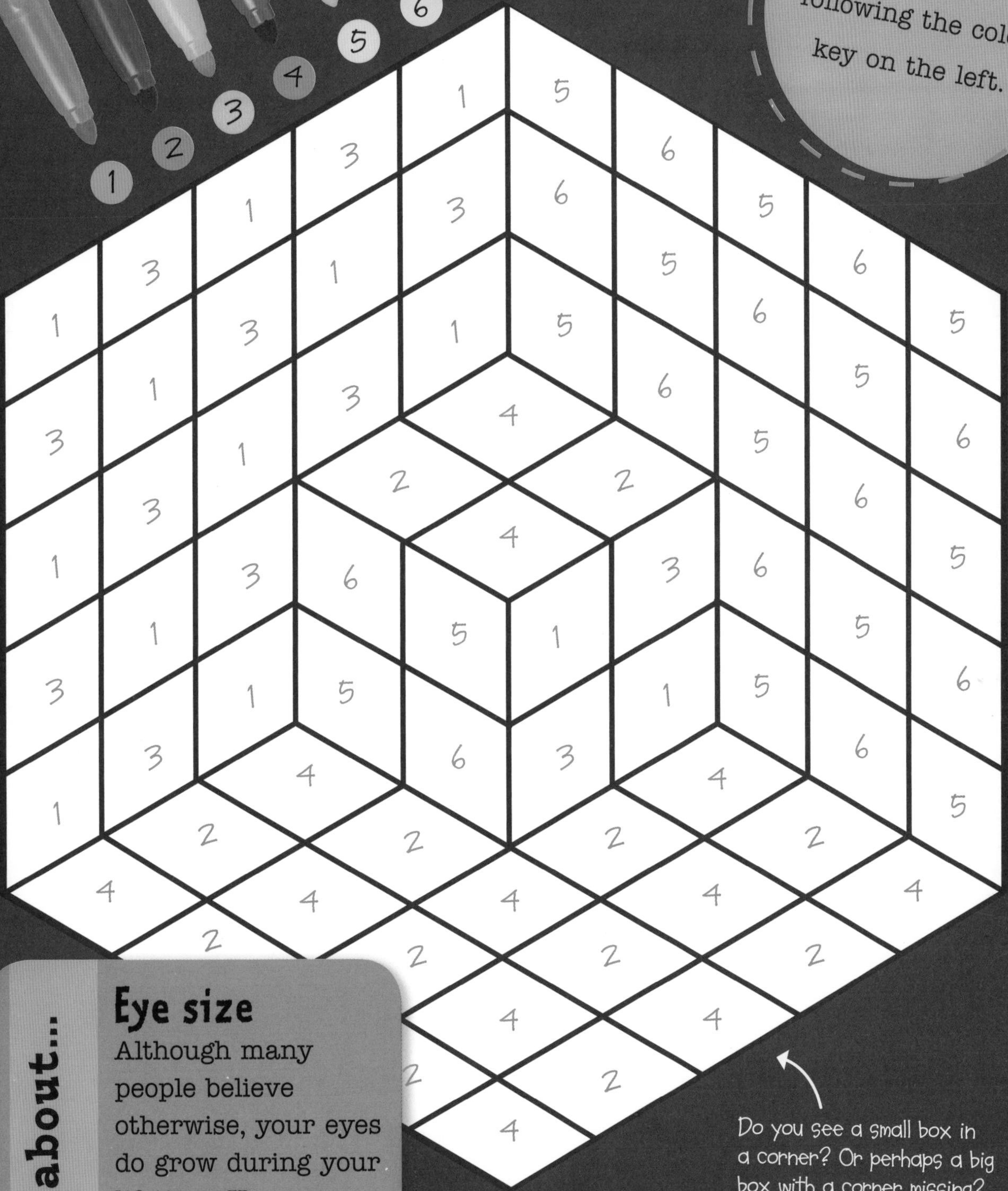

1 2 3 4 5 6

1 3 5
3 6
1 3 6 5
1 3 3 6 5 6
1 3 1 5 6 5
3 1 3 4 6 5 6
1 3 2 2 5 6 5
3 1 3 6 4 3 6 6
1 3 6 5 1 3 6 5
3 1 5 6 3 1 5 6
1 3 4 6 3 4 5
1 2 2 2 2
4 4 4 4 4
2 2 2 2
4 4
2 2
4

Facts about...

Eye size

Although many people believe otherwise, your eyes do grow during your lifetime. However, they reach their full size **earlier** in life than most parts of your body.

Do you see a small box in a corner? Or perhaps a big box with a corner missing?

FIND
the missing stickers and stick them into the right spots.

1 The flap, or the **pinna**, is the only part of the ear that we can see. Its main job is to catch and funnel soundwaves.

2 The waves travel through the tube-shaped **ear canal**, like a train going through a tunnel.

Take a look in ear

Listen! Can you hear that? We're always surrounded by noise, even if you don't notice it. Sound travels through the air as invisible waves. But how do our ears turn them into the things we hear?

Having two ears helps us tell the direction of sound. We can work out where a sound is coming from if it is louder in one ear than the other.

Under 40 decibels

40–70 decibels

Hear that?

Humans are amazing. We can detect even the tiniest sound, such as a pin dropping. But did you know there's a way to measure how loud a noise is? Sound is measured in **decibels** (**dB** for short).

Anything under 40dB is considered "quiet." The sound of leaves rustling is about 20dB.

When chatting with your friends (as long as you're not too loud) you'll make around 60dB of noise.

3 The waves of sound hit the paper-thin layer of skin called the **eardrum**, causing it to vibrate.

The ears aren't just for hearing. Liquid in the inner ear helps you to balance.

The ear bones are the smallest bones in your whole body.

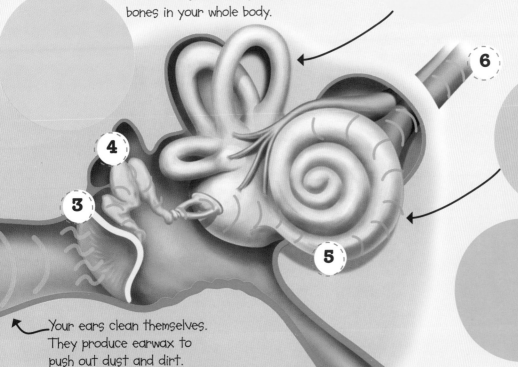

The liquid in the cochlea ripples, just like waves on water.

Your ears clean themselves. They produce earwax to push out dust and dirt.

An average person produces enough earwax in a year to fill a small cup!

4 This makes three tiny **ear bones** vibrate, too. They transmit waves into the snail-shaped liquid-filled cochlea.

5 The vibrations ripple through the liquid in the **cochlea**. Thousands of tiny hairlike fibers sense the movement.

6 The cells inside the cochlea send a sound message to the brain along a special hearing **nerve**.

70–90 decibels

90–120 decibels

120 decibels +

Sounds over 120dB can be harmful. Rocket launches are so loud their sound waves can damage buildings.

Anything higher than 70dB is "loud." This includes many household items, such as hair dryers and alarm clocks.

This is "extremely loud." A chainsaw noise can damage your ears in 2 minutes. Sound mufflers should be worn.

Taste buddies

Humans don't experience taste with just their tongues. They also use their sense of touch and smell to understand the flavor of their food.

Food aromas enter your nose as you eat and drink.

Smell

Special cells in your nose can recognize food aromas.

Nasal chamber

Mouth

The aromas also enter your nose through your throat.

Tongue

Touch

The insides of your mouth can sense the texture of different foods.

Throat

Taste

The taste buds on your tongue detect different tastes.

To the stomach

To the lungs

This fold is called the **epiglottis** (epa–glot–is). It closes when you eat to prevent food from entering your lungs.

Try...

chewing your food while pinching your nostrils together. Does it affect what you can taste?

When your nose is blocked food aromas can't enter, and so you can't smell what you are eating. This blocks an important part of the tasting process.

What is taste?

There are five types of **taste** that our tongues can recognize. These are **bitter**, **salty**, **sweet**, **sour**, and **savory** (or **umami**). The subtle differences in foods' flavors are mainly detected by our noses.

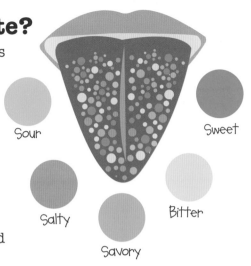

Sour

Sweet

Salty

Bitter

Savory

Facts about...

Your brain can remember 1 trillion (1,000,000,000,000) different smells.

The **look and sound** of food can make it taste better. Do you enjoy potato chips more when you hear them crunch?

They're bright red and have a smooth, firm surface. Their watery insides often burst out when you bite into them.

These bright—yellow fruits taste very sour and acidic. They have a hard and waxy surface, but are juicy in the middle.

This wobbly, colorful dessert has a solid shape. It melts in your mouth when you eat it, and it smells and tastes very sweet.

STICK

the food stickers in place that match the descriptions above each plate.

The outer skin is wrinkly and soft. The white flesh beneath tears easily into strips and has a savory, meaty flavor.

Soft and spongy, this food tastes and smells very sweet. It is often yellow and can be decorated with colorful, sugary toppings.

This shiny fruit is round and crunchy. The white flesh tastes sharp and sour, although its juice tastes sweet.

Touchy feely

There are many different sensations that you can feel using your sense of touch. This is because there are lots of different types of touch sensors beneath your skin.

Feel all around

Your sense of touch is the only one of the five main senses that you can feel anywhere on your body. This is because touch sensations are detected all over your skin.

You feel **pain** when your skin cells are being damaged.

Temperature tells you not to touch something too hot or cold!

Light touch is caused by soft objects.

Near the surface

These sensations are all detected by sensors near the skin's surface.

Pressure is felt when something presses hard on your skin.

Stretching is felt when your skin is pulled.

Vibration is caused by something shaking quickly.

STICK

in place the stickers showing pictures of objects that can cause these sensations.

Deep beneath

Receptors found deeper beneath the skin detect these sensations.

How sensitive?

Some parts of the body are more sensitive than others because they have more touch sensors. A special drawing called a **touch homunculus** shows which parts of the body are most sensitive by showing them larger than normal.

The ears are more sensitive than you might think.

I've got a good feeling about this!

The hands are particularly sensitive to light touch.

The lips are very sensitive to hot and cold.

The tongue's sense of touch helps us feel our food.

The fingertips have more sensors than any other part of the body.

The toes are the most sensitive part of the feet.

STICK the body part stickers in place to turn this image into a touch homunculus.

Finger trick

Put one finger in cold water, one in warm. Now put both in room-temperature water. The room-temperature water will feel cold to the warm-water finger and hot to the cold-water finger.

COLD

ROOM Temperature

WARM

Other reflexes...

MATCH
each reflex with the correct explanation. Write the number in the box.

1 This reaction happens when you are cold. It's your body's way of warming you up.

2 Your body does this when something comes near your eyes. It protects them from damage.

3 If something gets stuck in your throat, your body does this to clear the path to the lungs so you can breathe easily.

4 Germs build up in your nose, and this is how the body removes them.

Coughing

Shivering

Blinking

Sneezing

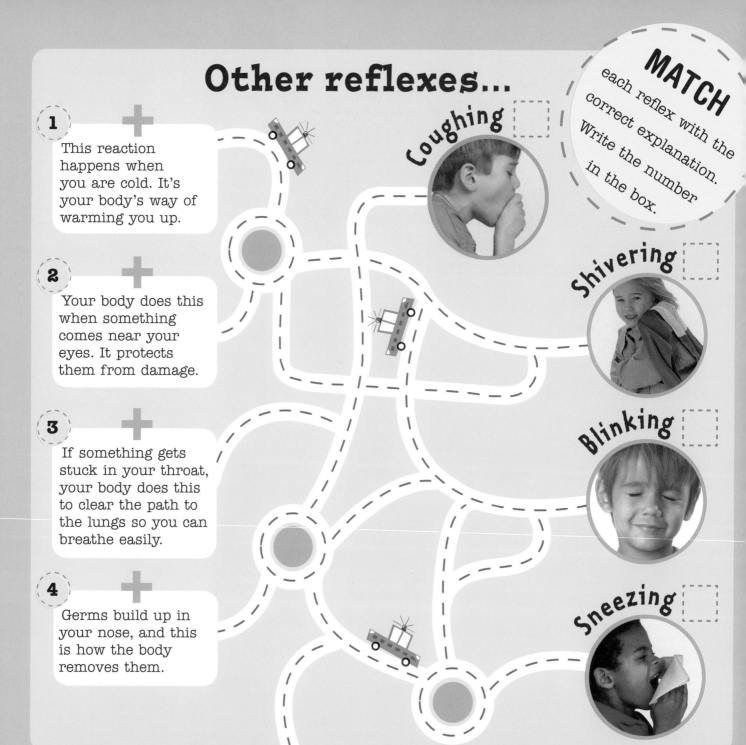

Facts about...

Speedy signals
The signals in your nerves are tiny bursts of electric energy. These signals travel through your nerves at 250mph (400kph)—that's faster than a race car!

Ouch!
Emergency!
Oops!

The hand senses a sharp pain!

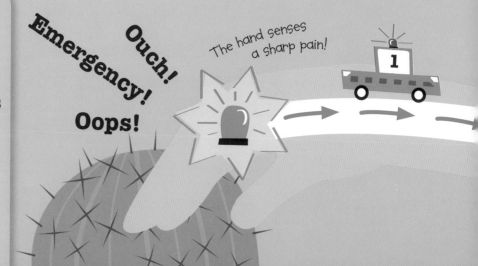

Emergency reflexes

The body often protects us by reacting to danger before we realize it's there. This automatic reaction to something that might harm you is called a **reflex**.

Brain

Your brain becomes aware of the pain after you've already moved away from the source.

A pain signal travels up to the brain.

3

The spinal cord receives the warning, sending out motor and pain signals.

Spinal cord

Quick reactions

Normally the muscles are instructed to move by the brain. However, when the body senses danger, nerves in the spinal cord react quickly and send signals telling the muscles to move the body out of harm's way. Because the signals don't have to travel to the brain, the reaction is quicker.

1 Warning signal **2** Motor signal **3** Pain signal

It sends a warning signal along the nerves to the spine.

2

The motor signal travels along another nerve to the muscles, telling them to move the hand out of danger.

47

Hormone controls

FIND the missing stickers and stick them in place.

Hormones are chemicals that take messages all over the body through the bloodstream. They let your body know when you're feeling sleepy, hungry, or scared.

Feeling sleepy?

Melatonin is a hormone that kicks in when it starts to get dark. It signals when it's time to go to bed and let's your whole body know to prepare for sleep.

Feeling hungry?

The stomach produces "hunger hormone," called **ghrelin**. Its top job is to tell the brain when you're hungry. The levels go down after you eat a meal or a snack.

Feeling scared?

Your **hands** may shake and your palms sweat.

You will get an oxygen boost and more air will go to your **lungs**.

Your tummy can feel fluttery because more blood is going to the lungs and muscles and less blood is flowing to the **stomach**.

Your **pupils** (centers of your eyes) will become larger and more open.

Your **mouth** may feel dry.

The **heart** will beat faster.

Epinephrine is a hormone produced in response to an unexpected or stressful situation. It gives you a rapid energy boost. In caveman times the extra energy would have helped you to run away from or fight a predator.

Epinephrine is not only produced when you are scared—it can also be because of a thrill. Your body makes epinephrine for many reasons.

Or, when you are about to start a race.

Your epinephrine might be high before you take a test at school!

It could be when you see a scary spider!

Or if you're on a rollercoaster.

DRAW what would make your epinephrine levels rise.

Amazing human

From fighting infections and repairing cuts to growing, the human body is amazing. In this chapter we look at some of the astonishing things your body can do.

Don't forget to put your stickers in first.

Page _____

Page _____

Page _____

FIND these pictures on pages 52–64 and write the page numbers in the boxes.

Page _____

Page _____

Page _____

What do we do that animals don't?

There are lots of different animals in the world, but humans seem very different from the rest. Here are some things that we do that other animals don't.

Your feet have grown!

1 Humans have **long childhoods**. Many animals can walk within a day of being born, but it can take humans up to a year!

2 **Blushing** can reveal what we feel, even against our wishes. No other animals do this in quite the same way.

...I read about it online

Did you hear what happened?..

3 Many animals communicate with others of their kind, but only humans are capable of **speech.**

COLOR in the picture of animals doing human activities.

4 Some animals use sticks as tools, but only humans have **complex technology.**

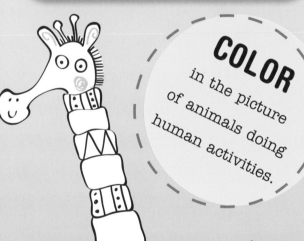

It's handy being able to hold so many bags!

5 Many animals have furry coats to keep warm, but only humans wear **clothes**.

6 Having an **upright posture** allows us to use our hands comfortably while moving around.

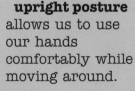

51

Growing up

As you grow, your body and mind get bigger and more skilled. This means the tasks you can perform get more and more complex.

STICK

Stick a sticker for each in a sticker draw what age. Then draw like you might look like as a teenager.

12–17 years

By 12 you will be nearly in your teens. You will go to middle school and be much more independent. By 17 you will have almost grown to your full height and will start to look like an adult.

9–11 years

This girl loves playing sports and enjoys being part of a team. When she is on her own she likes to read or draw pictures.

6–8 years

This boy loves to play catch and ride his bike with his best friend. He is always taking things apart to see how they work.

2–3 years

Now a preschooler, this little girl can hop, run, and jump. She dresses herself before nursery school in the morning.

9–18 months

Learning to stand and walk, this baby girl can feed herself. She likes pictures of babies and loves to see herself in the mirror.

4–5 years

This little boy is active and imaginative. He likes to dress up in costumes and invent games. He has started to read and write.

18–24 months

This little toddler can now walk by himself and has started to use a few words. He has begun to play with other kids at nursery school.

0–9 months

This baby can sit up on her own and is now starting to crawl around. Peekaboo is her favorite game.

Fueling the body

Your body gets its fuel from the food you eat. Eating a variety of foods from all the food groups will give you enough energy to be active, grow, and learn.

READ about the different food groups and stick in the foods using the clues to help.

Brown Rice

White Rice

Pasta

Oats

Brown bread with fiber is digested slowly, so keeps you going longer

Fill up the jars!

Stick your favorite fruits and vegetables on this shelf

Fruits and Vegetables

Vegetables and fruits are full of important **vitamins** and **minerals**. They also contain **fiber** to help with digestion and chemicals that **protect the body's cells from harm**. Try to eat plenty of fruits and vegetables every day.

Fill the bowl with fruit and eat a rainbow.

Did you know? Different colored fruits and vegetables contain different vitamins.

Green vegetables are full of antioxidants that protect your cells from damage.

Orange fruits and vegetables contain carotene. This helps keep your eyesight clear and sharp.

Green vegetables

Orange fruits and vegetables

Dairy

Dairy products are foods that contain milk, such as cheese and yogurt. These foods are full of **calcium**, which is needed to build **strong teeth and bones**. They also help the nerves and muscles work well.

Carbohydrates

Carbohydrates, such as bread, rice, and oats, supply **energy** to all your cells. It is best to eat whole-grain carbohydrates, such as brown bread or pasta. They release energy slowly throughout the day.

Choose the dairy foods you would like to put in the fridge.

Eggs contain high-quality protein, great for building muscle.

Fish is high in the good fat omega 3, which may help improve your memory and ability to learn.

Sweet treats

Your body doesn't really need sugar or unhealthy fats, but they can taste very nice. Too much of these can cause health problems, so they should only be eaten as an occasional treat.

Cookies

Candy

Proteins

All your cells are made of protein. Eating protein, such as meat, eggs, beans, legumes, and nuts, helps to make sure your body can repair cells and build new ones.

Oils

Fill the jars and cans with proteins.

Fats

Your body needs fats in small amounts, but they need to be the right kinds of fats. Healthy fats are found in fish, nuts, avocado, and olive oil.

Nuts

Lentils

What's in a dream?

Although sleeping is something we spend over a third of our lives doing, it is something we know very little about. One thing we can often remember about our time asleep is our dreams.

Are you an owl or a lark?

Different people are more active at different times of the day. **Larks** are people who get up early, while night **owls** are people who stay up late. **Hummingbirds** fit somewhere between the two. Take the quiz to find out which category you fit into.

Stick a sticker here for the column that got the highest score (you can stick in two if it was a draw).

Check the box that most applies to you for each question.

	Lark	Hummingbird	Owl
Do you need an alarm clock?	I wake up early on my own! ☐	I sometimes set an alarm ☐	I have to set two alarms! ☐
What's your favorite time of day to exercise?	Morning ☐	Afternoon ☐	Evening ☐
How do you feel in the morning?	Ready to go! ☐	It takes a while to get going ☐	Bearish—don't talk to me! ☐
How do you feel in the evening	Falling asleep ☐	Getting sleepy ☐	Full of beans! ☐
Do you often take a nap during the day?	Never! ☐	Sometimes ☐	Whenever I can! ☐

Add up your checkmarks. Which column got the highest score?

It's all in your head!

Some people claim to be able to control some of their dreams. This is because they realize that they are dreaming while in a dream, and so attempt to change it. This is called **lucid dreaming**.

Maybe you really wanted something to happen in a dream and then it did?

Have you ever had a dream that you control?

What would you try and do if you realized you could change your dreams?

DRAW

a picture of a dream you have had, or invent a new dream for this sleeping person.

Draw your dream here

Z Z Z Z Z Z Z Z Z Z Z

Facts about...

How long?

The recommended amount of sleep for children ages 5 to 9 is between **10 and 11 hours** per night. Babies should sleep for 16 hours, and adults between 7 and 8 hours.

STICK the stickers in place, then draw and describe your own germ.

Horrible infections

Germs are tiny nasties that get into your body and make you sick. Different kinds of germ cause different illnesses. Here are a few you may have heard about.

Facts about...

Which type?

There are several different types of germ. Two common ones are **viruses** and **bacteria**. Bacteria can be killed using special drugs called **antibiotics**, but these do not work on viruses.

A good sneeze shoots me 16 ft (5 meters)!

Common cold (Virus)

Symptoms: Headache, sneezing, coughing, sore throat

Treatment: Rest, fluids

Prevention: Wash your hands to reduce risk of infection

Fact: Green snot is full of white blood cells. These gather in your nose to fight cold viruses.

What comes out when you sneeze?

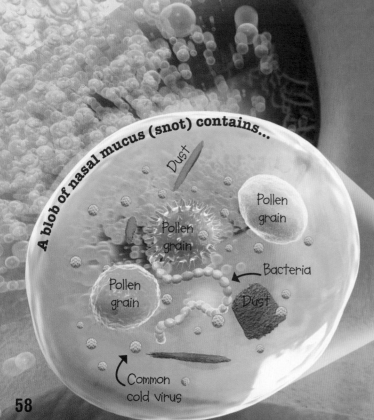

A blob of nasal mucus (snot) contains...

Dust

Pollen grain

Pollen grain

Pollen grain

Bacteria

Dust

Common cold virus

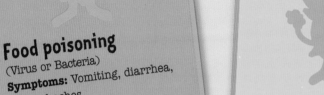

My name is E. coli. I live in raw meat and dirty water.

You can fit 1 million bacteria onto the point of a pencil!

Acne (Bacteria)

Symptoms: Tiny, red or yellow, pus-filled spots

Treatment: Good hygiene, acne medicine

Prevention: Unknown

Fact: Around 85 percent of people in US between the ages of 12 and 24 have or have had acne.

Food poisoning

(Virus or Bacteria)

Symptoms: Vomiting, diarrhea, stomachaches

Treatment: Rest, drink water

Prevention: Wash your hands before eating and preparing food

Fact: Caused by germs such as **salmonella**, **norovirus**, and **E. coli**.

Warts (Virus)

Symptoms: Solid, cauliflower-like growths on skin

Treatment: Cream, freezing

Prevention: Avoid touching warts

Fact: Although warts heal and disappear, the virus will always remain inside an infected person's body.

Draw a new virus or bacteria

Name: ....

Symptoms: ....

....

Measles (Virus)

Symptoms: Fever, coughing, red eyes, spreading rash

Treatment: None

Prevention: Vaccination (shot)

Fact: Most children get a measles shot when they are babies. This has dramatically reduced cases of measles.

Dirty hands are a great place for a bacteria party.

Tonsillitis (Bacteria)

Symptoms: Large swellings at the back of the mouth, fever, sore throat

Treatment: Rest, fluids. In some cases antibiotic drugs are needed.

Prevention: None

Fact: Tonsillitis is often caused by the bacteria **Streptococcus** and is sometimes called **strep throat**.

Body under attack!

Your body fights infections with an army of white blood cells. They find and destroy viruses and bacteria that get inside you before you become sick.

T cell

T cells are white blood cells that look for anything unusual inside your body, including germs. If they find any, they tell B cells to destroy them.

B cell

B cells are white blood cells that destroy germs and other unwanted items. They make antibodies that break down their targets.

Phagocytes

Phagocytes (fag-uh-sites) are white blood cells that look for germs and other dangers to eat and destroy.

SEARCH AND DESTROY

Viruses

Look for these **viruses** on the opposite page and stick **B cell** stickers in place over them.

Warts

Measles

Common cold

SEARCH AND DESTROY

Bacteria

Look for these bad **bacteria** on the opposite page and stick **phagocyte** stickers in place over them.

E. coli

Staphylococcus

Acne

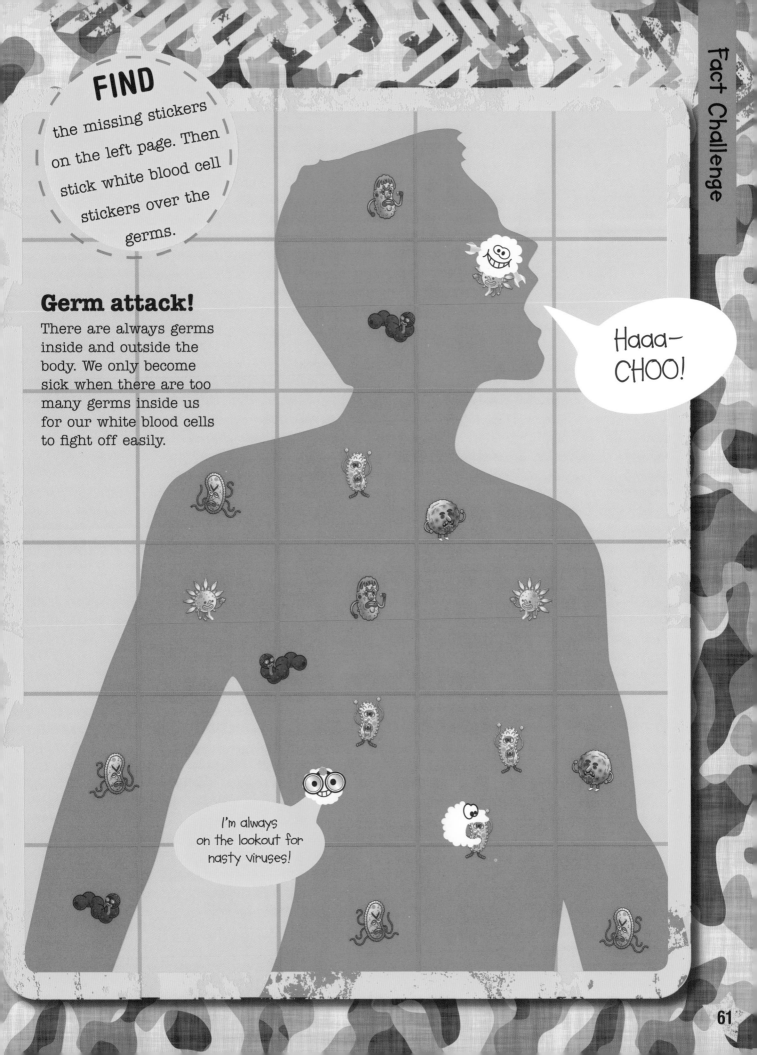

FIND

the missing stickers on the left page. Then stick white blood cell stickers over the germs.

Germ attack!

There are always germs inside and outside the body. We only become sick when there are too many germs inside us for our white blood cells to fight off easily.

Haaa-CHOO!

I'm always on the lookout for nasty viruses!

Platelets
in action

When you cut yourself, the body has a special process to heal the wound and avoid infection. Follow the stages to find out how it works.

COLOR in the rest of the pictures to show how the wound heals.

Red blood cell

Bacteria

3 White blood cells arrive to fight off any germs around the wound and prevent infection.

White blood cell

Skin cell

1 When you cut yourself, blood cells escape through the opening in your skin.

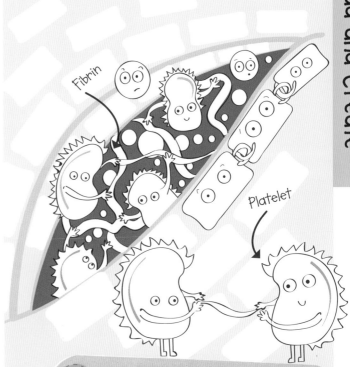

Fibrin

Platelet

2 **Platelets** (a special type of blood cell) help to create strings of protein called **fibrin** to help them block the opening.

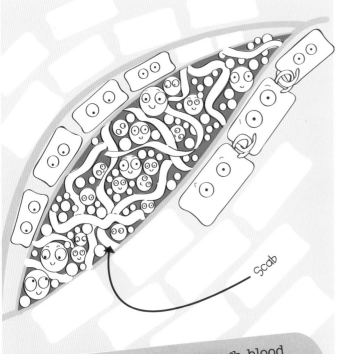

Scab

4 Soon there are enough blood cells and fibrin strands to form a scab and block the opening. New skin is formed beneath the scab.

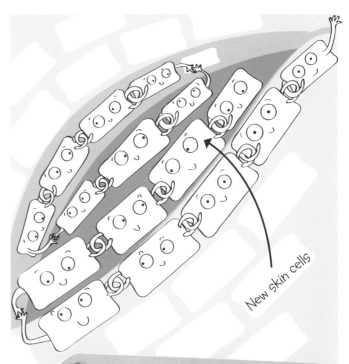

New skin cells

5 Eventually the scab falls off to reveal the new skin cells underneath. The cut is now healed.

FIND the stickers that correctly match the shapes below.

Strange but true?

There are many things to learn about the human body. The functions it performs can be both weird and wonderful and sometimes hard to believe!

1 You don't need gravity to swallow—astronauts can eat upside down in space.

2 If someone were touching your brain you wouldn't be able to feel it—that's because there are no touch receptors in your brain.

3 On average, people fart 14 times per day.

4 A healthy person produces up to 3 pints (1.5 liters) of saliva per day.

5 Nails grow faster in summer than they do in winter.

6 There are the same number of hairs on the human body as on a chimpanzee, although most human hairs are so small and thin that they are hardy noticed.

7 Bone is not the strongest substance in your body—the material your teeth are made of is.

Complete the skeleton on **pages 4–5** with these stickers.

These stickers belong on **page 7.**

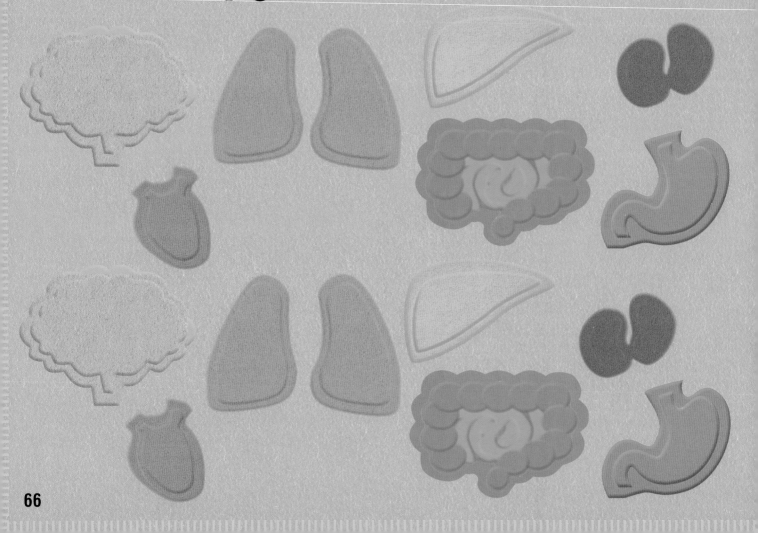

Add these stickers to **page 9.**

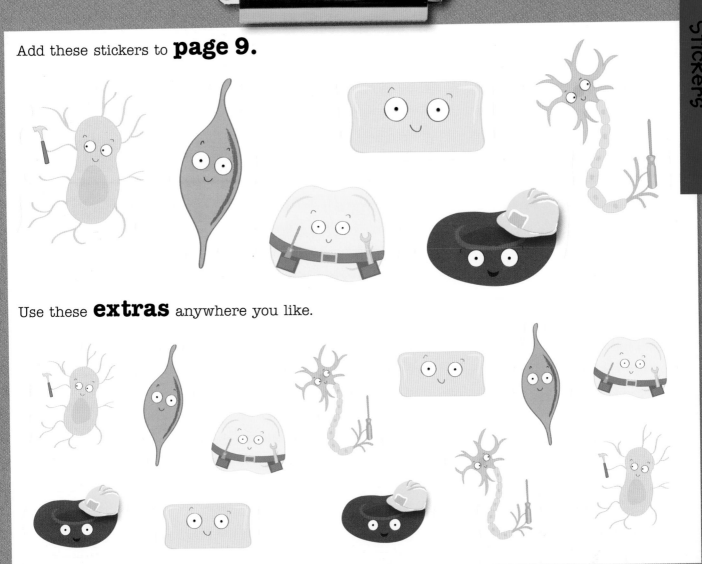

Use these **extras** anywhere you like.

These stickers are **extras**, too.

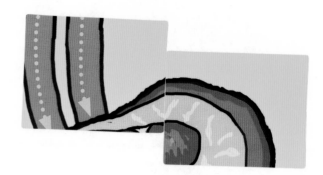

Use these **extras** anywhere you like.

Use these stickers to create complete X-rays on **page 16.**

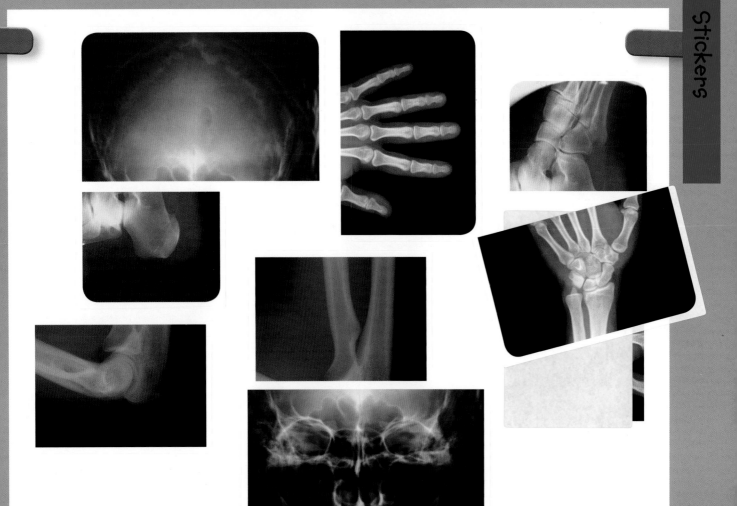

These stickers are **extras.**

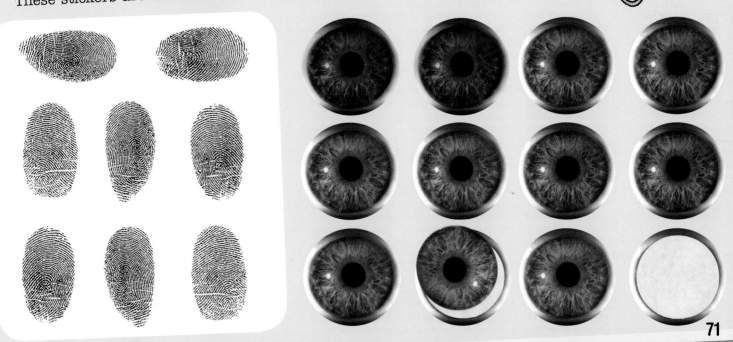

Use these to solve the heart puzzle on **page 23.** The other stickers are extras.

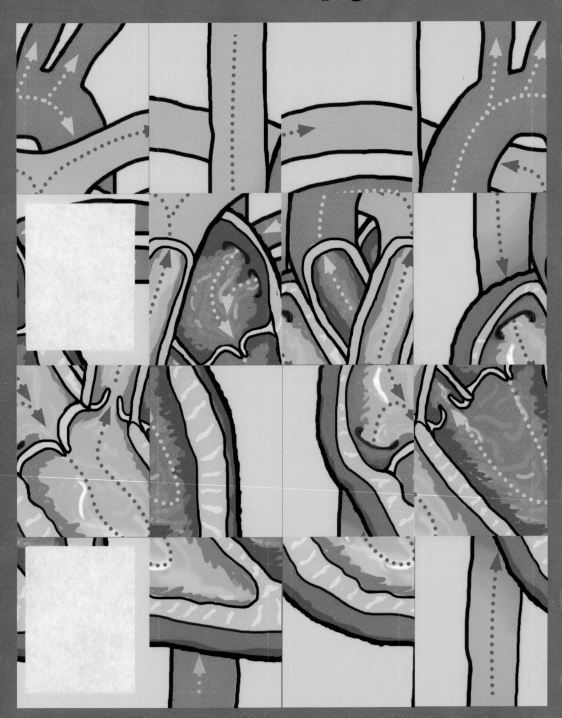

Use these **extra hearts** anywhere you like.

The big stickers go on **page 25.** The others are extras.

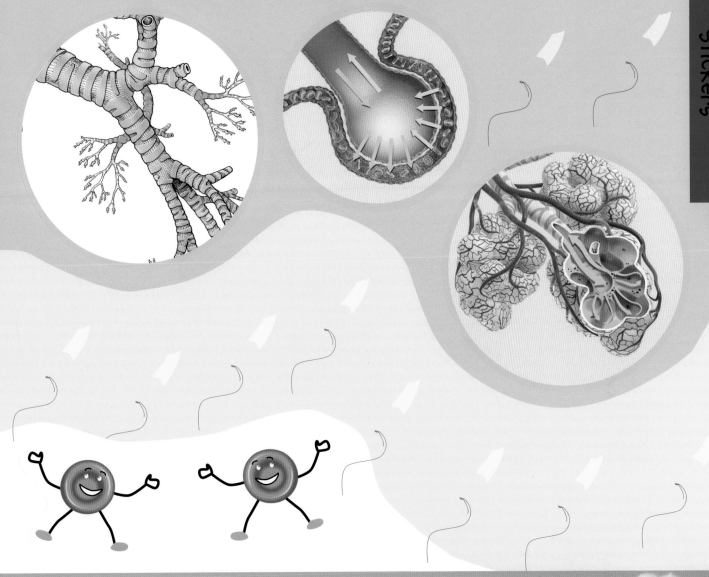

Match these stickers to the captions on **pages 28-29.**

Find the right spots for these stickers on **pages 30–31.**

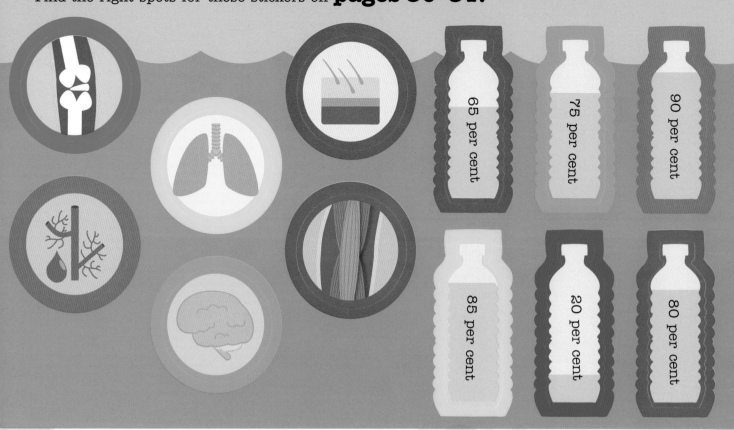

65 per cent

75 per cent

90 per cent

85 per cent

20 per cent

80 per cent

Use these **extra ones** anywhere you like.

78

These stickers belong on **page 32.**

Choose a hat!

Add rosy cheeks.

Add sunglasses if you want to.

Choose a hat!

Stick in the magnifying glass to show the skin up close.

Stick in these cold cheeks.

Add warm clothes.

These stickers are **extras**, too.

Add some accessories, too!

Use these **extra** stickers anywhere you like.

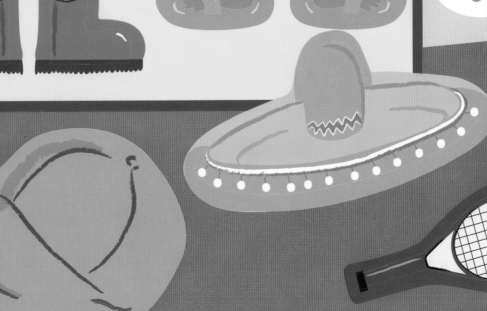

Use these **extra** stickers anywhere you like.

Place these stickers next to the matching captions on **page 41.**

These stickers go along the bottom of **pages 40–41.**

Hello

Hi

These belong on **page 43.**

These pictures of things you touch belong on **page 44.** The others are extras.

Use these body parts to complete the image on **page 45.** The others are extras.

These belong on **page 48.**

The animals are extra stickers!

These stickers go on **pages 54–55.**

Choose from these for **page 56.**

These stickers go on **pages 58–59.**

These stickers go on **pages 60–61.**

These belong on **page 64.**

Saliva

1.5 litres